Nostalgia for a Trumpet

Poems of Memory & History

SUSAN
D.
ANDERSON

TÍA CHUCHA PRESS
LOS ANGELES

To my son, Langston,
all of my family,
friends and b.w.

ACKNOWLEDGMENTS

Several of these poems have appeared, some in earlier versions, in publications including *5 AM; The Antioch Review; Art Against Racism/L'Art Contre Le Racisme* (an international exhibition in Vancouver, B.C.); *The Black Scholar; Electrum; Fast Talk/Full Volume: An Anthology of African American Poetry; First Intensity; Life in L.A.: A Portfolio of Women's Writing; The Massachusetts Review; Obras; ONTHEBUS; rara avis; Ten Contemporary American Poets;* and *Xavier Review.*

BOOK DESIGN: Jane Brunette
COVER PHOTOS: Courtesy of the Southern California Library for Social Studies and Research. (USC Digital Archive - Couple prepare to cut their wedding cake, Oct. 29, 1943, Los Angeles. USC Digital Archive - U.S. Negro troops in action, April 1945, Germany.) ADDITIONAL BACK COVER PHOTO: Courtesy of Dunbar Economic Development Corporation. (Socialites.)

PUBLISHED BY:
Tía Chucha Press
A Project of Tía Chucha's Centro Cultural
PO Box 328
San Fernando, CA 91341
www.tiachucha.com

DISTRIBUTED BY:
Northwestern University Press
Chicago Distribution Center
11030 South Langley Avenue
Chicago, IL 60628

Tía Chucha Press is supported by the National Endowment for the Arts and operating funds from Tía Chucha's Centro Cultural. Tía Chucha's Centro Cultural have received support from the Los Angeles Department of Cultural Affairs, Los Angeles Community Redevelopment Agency, Thrill Hill Foundation, the Center for Cultural Innovation, the Middleton Foundation, Not Just Us Foundation, the Liberty Hill Foundation, Youth Can Service, Toyota Sales, Solidago Foundation, Panta Rhea Foundation and other grants and donors including Bruce Springsteen, John Densmore, Dan Attias, Dave Marsh, Denise Chávez and John Randall of the Border Book Festival, Luis & Trini Rodríguez, Adrienne Rich, Richard Foos, Mel Gilman, Tom Hayden and others.

CONTENTS

Music

Lament

Elsewhere

City

Bliss

Music

Hearing Charles Lloyd at MOCA

For b.w.

Exhausted from my failures
I arrive

Downtown
Where birds circle
The trembling mirror
Faces of skyscrapers

Evening doesn't fall
It rises

Stars sudden and complete
The day ends with You
In your no hat elegance

Time tree rings
My skin with age
And laments sour
The years

You stand brightly next to me
The pavement holds
Our sacred weight

Song touches your bare head
In the dusk crowd
Of saxophone thirsty
Jazz lovers

Nostalgia for a Trumpet

(Or, when I'm Reincarnated,
I Want to Come Back as Louis Armstrong)

I wanted the kind of life
That would leave me
Dreaming in the gin fumes
After King Oliver's Creole Band
Had prompted the yearning out of everyone
And left them like that
Clean

I wanted to be able
To blow a canal wind through brass
And make Basin Street hungry

I wanted to be the one
Tooting out Fat Tuesday ecstasy
In a wealth of dancing arms
And the warnings of hips
Piper
Who would be the one remembered
For breaking the heat barrier

Cabaret

FROM A PHOTOGRAPH OF THE HARLEM RENAISSANCE

I got a fur coat
So T.B. don't bother me
Lucky these New Negroes
Got money to spend
And the whites?
I don't live downtown
But downtown's been where I been

No hot chocolates in this review
These girls are on their way!
Some of them gone to white Harlem
Paris
The other day

It takes a while for the dance
In all ten of us to die
Arms linked, breast to breast
I wear the "H" on my chest
Knees aligned, tap shoes pointed
Ballet style
Both legs in full view, blonde flesh
"Ripe bananas"
The photographer tests
And blusters with drapes and shutters
"Yeah, now smile"

Lightning strikes our balmy grins
Immortalized in zinc
"Later"
"Yeah, same place, honey"
"Back to work again"

Morning's the only Harlem I ever see
Tania root, crystal fines
Strolling the stands, black eye peas
Won't see the Obi man today
This storied place is on my mind
And sleep is blocks away

Started off a bad year
Marcus Garvey in prison
Club owner, Boss Wilkins, dead
Yellow Johnny disappeared
Smoking like the murder weapon
He blasted through Boss' head

Kid left me

For a while I was a maid
Teaching a white lady how to dance
My trade's an exotic secret
In her circumstance
Charleston
She could never get it down
Lucky for her, I always thought
She lives downtown

An Explanation

The New York Times reported
In 1923

An incident in France
That you can plainly see

Was a clash of understanding
Between the French police
And, *oui*, some American Negroes
Who were sad enough, indeed

They strode along the Seine
In the funeral of a friend

The friend had asked a jazz band
The best in Paris
To send him off in style
Beyond the *Champs-Élysée*

The New York Times insisted
In 1923

That the mourners began to foxtrot
In a spirit wild and free

The French police were scandalized
(In the words of the New York Times)
Civilization was a stake
If Negroes danced at funerals
A spectacle they would make

The band agreed to slow
The cadence in which it played
The mourners then all one-stepped
On the way to their friend's grave

The man was buried
But the not the way he asked
All went home
Sad at the interruption of their task

Now, it's important
First of all, to say
These mourners were not fox trotting
That wasn't their way

This was no ballroom floor
Or speakeasy den
It was a Negro funeral
With its own tradition

The shame may have been averted
If the police had understood

After years and years of sorrow
Grief has a special mood
It can make you feel so bad
That you start to feeling good

You're alive, after all
You have to be to mourn
On that wisdom, a principle was born

Your friend is lying still
He can never move again
But life is in your body
And it has a will

So, you hold on to life
With everything you got
You move it, toss it, shake it, baby

But, break it, you do not

It wasn't a dance then
That the policemen stopped
But the Negroes saying *au revoir*
In the way that life has taught

New Orleans Funeral Music

Makes you want to hear a cornet wail

The Grand Marshall slows
His rampart way in black
Coat tails seeking the dust
In elderly travail
His step keeps rhythm
With the weeping carriage
No Smile Joe driving
(Himself a specter
Beneath the death plume sail)

Makes you want to die yourself

The shoulders move forward
When the feet cross back
There is a measure to the mourning
Hesitation
A momentary lack of faith
In the Resurrection
That blithe swing back to life
And the pig foot banquet
Expected later that night

Makes you want to die right

Some People Just Can't Handle Fame

Backstage Big Mama Thornton
Insists it will be you, Johnny Ace
Who takes Rhythm and Blues
Over the peak
You'll be so big
The ocean won't even be able to hold you,
And you don't care that Big Mama can't be trusted
Because you, Johnny Ace, are prettier than she is
And she is in love
With that

All you want this Christmas Eve in 1954
Is the promise kept

You tilt the tall bourbon
Down your throat
And pick up the gun
All chambers empty
Except the one
Filled like your heart
With expectation

The sweat on your head
Floods the conked
Roots of your hair shining
Under the dressing room mirror
Lights bright as the Christmas star
Noises from the Houston crowd
Blare through

You pull the trigger

You know what will happen
They won't let you sing yourself
Clean

It is what they insist
On giving back to you
You offer your sweet profile
At the piano
A bit of your smooth face
To the crowd
And flowers are thrown
On the stage
You let your voice
Fly beyond your doubts
And a woman in the audience
Sighs
Taking everyone with her
To heaven
You beg in your song
For forgiveness
And they find their own salvation

You pull the trigger

This time
Your reflection drops
From the backstage mirror
Like a sight gag
The .22 pistol lies
On the floor
A heart pumped out
Big Mama kneels over you
Her own heart thrusting
Like a bullet

But all the hollering
In the world
Won't kill the silence

# Before She Died

In Memory of Big Mama Thornton

The queen plotted
To end the cancer ridden
Interregnum
Of her years gone bad
Her tantrums
About the king stealing
Hound Dog from her
The exile years
Sipping milky Scotch
Alone in her living room
Under the ceiling plaster
That hung down
In great, stained flags
Of the Blues Nation

She makes her comeback
At the Club Lingerie
In Hollywood
Fierce voice rocketed
Into the Milky Way
By Buddy Guy's guitar
In the final number
Gravity forces her
To the wooden stool
She weeps at her landing
Sips her glass filled with courage
Take your time, Big Mama
Take your time
No way to talk to a queen
"I don't rush myself for nothing.
I wait till the rush gets to me."

Johnny Otis had taken the girl
Six feet tall, hefty with song
From behind the mule plow
In the Alabama mud
Put her in Carnegie Hall
The night she was crowned
In a silk gown sewn with stars
She walked her voice softly
Under the music
Then ran it to a frenzy
Lost in the rough crossing
She kicked up her feet
And her dirty men's boots told all
About her mother dying
When the girl was fourteen
Told all about the men
And the jook joints
And her fate in the blues
Told all
About the little school girl
Swinging it on home
Little school girl, little angel
Gone, gone, gone, gone, gone

At her funeral
It was told how the queen
Surrounded by her court
Played a last hand of whist
Until the milk in her glass
Couldn't keep up with the Scotch
When she laid her head
Against the sway back couch
Somebody, looking at
The song wasted body
Caving cheeks, gaunt chin
Under the Stetson brim,
Somebody said,
"Big Mama ain't big no more."
The ages passed

Life paused in the moment called dusk
Night entered the living room
Like kin folk
Coming just to sit a while

A Nice Dude from L.A.

IN MEMORY OF CHARLES MINGUS FROM A LINE IN HIS AUTOBIOGRAPHY,
BENEATH THE UNDERDOG

Rancho La Tajuata where did you go?
When Mingus the infant grew to a man among
The traqueras and Pullman porters and whites
On the Ku Klux Klan scarred asphalt sinkhole
Streets of paradise now called Watts
So began cultivation of the legend, the notoriety
And thorough surprise
Of the world's only black working class avant-garde workshop
Continually producing unprecedented goods "Made in Watts"
New jazz, new sculpture, new painting,
New urgency because somebody had
To save art, revive it during that Leave It to Beaver time
When white men dribbled on canvases and fronted for
The State Department and committed suicide because they knew
Abstract Expressionism was a lie
Told so that Frigidaire could sell more deep freezes
And white people could be the only ones who qualified
For federal home loans and the height of culture
Was redundancy and the NBC Television Symphony Orchestra
For Commie-hating suburbanites
So, Watts burned. Its brilliance was white hot. Astounding.
Sculpture of debris and memory:
Purifoy. Outterbridge. Riddle.
So many knights and ladies with their metal, electronic breasts
Their visor eyes searching the fragments for meaning, finding the lost
books, the urban desert text that tells us who we are.
So this shit piece of South L.A. recalibrated
The way the earth turns on its axis.
Nobody cared.
Even though Don Cherry, Eric Dolphy and Ornette Coleman
Talked to him soothing in brass exploration of the native Watts tongue,
Mingus couldn't take it.

The storefronts spilled passion onto the pavement
Little houses in Watts playing imitation of life on TV
Single family homes where the Cleavers didn't live
And which the Cleavers couldn't think about, because all those mind pictures
Of Mexicans and Negroes in Watts might put some
Vitamins and fiber into the Cleaver's Wonder Bread
And dinner would never be the same.
Houses about as big as a railroad car
Jaundiced lawns that can't
Get enough water in this concrete habitat
Crypt for the river L.A.
The houses sprouted weed-like in the grip and grimace
Of talking steel mills. Those were the good old days
When the air choked you with the busy smoke of
All the nearby factories and the cancer stink of the oil refineries
Born on wings of heaven from the harbor at the lavish Pacific edge.
A job was just blocks away.
But too many times the LAPD cracked your head
On the exuberant way home alcohol-fueled because
Work wasn't a joke – Would you like to haul metal
Or cook rubber or take your big man hands and instead
Of the poem sliding around in your brain, make an automobile?

Simon Rodia was the only one with patience.
The pavement burned in the inevitable heat
A forgotten scrap kindled under broken glass
Still life: The Neighborhood as Empty Lot
Subject to Arson.
The relatives in Texas heard about those good old days
And they wouldn't stop coming to L.A., just to try it out.
Don't ever say that Watts isn't a destination, boy was it ever,
And just like before – when the brother G.I.s came home
And none of the banks would lend them money
To make a home a man could be proud of,
And none of the stores wanted you walking
Through the front door, and none of the restaurants
Wanted your black ass on a seat in sight,
Even though this wasn't a war for mankind,

This was a war for the means of manufacturing
And gross national product and international trade
And global dominance – the Negroes were willing,
Eager, sometimes happy to help. So they came to Watts
And there just weren't enough little houses and the sewage
Was always backing up and you had to drive a half hour
To catch the freeway north and the god damn cops
Knew you were a darky migrant, so on the way home from work
They whipped you twice as bad as the natives.

Legend has it that Marquette, Ron and Mama Frye went nuts
On an overused street corner under a bad moon.
Right around then, the jazz police cut his performance in Monterey
And Mingus showed up, just like that, in LA.
He could still smell fire on the breeze.
"Don't Let It Happen Here" his song demanded.
But the plea from his studio was too late.
Everybody knows that August is the worst month in L.A.
When the heat waves rise from the earthquake cracks
And we are not the French
And Los Angeles is not Paris and we remain here
To keep the sun company during its most extreme,
Its cosmic show down with incipient autumn
In the Santa Ana winds that tangle over the mountains
And struggle with the ocean air and cause
The vapor of nightmares hanging over the city
Madness.

Thou hast a voice, great city, not understood by all.
Mingus was the wise, great and good that Shelley wrote about
He was a genius and he was angry, Watts personified.
So Mingus left, and forgot to turn off the gas
He left embers fuming in the furnace.
All those years gone, he had so much to think about: the way
The city spoke in growls and chants. The ice moon
Cutting the flesh of night air. Jazz, elusive prayer,
Whore, strutting a fantasy between her legs, wandering
The lyric, giving her soul to drink
For the hot place in your belly.

Even in this dungeon of streets she questions, breathes
In the skin and muscle of your bass.
This is the work then, no matter where you are:
To become a voice within a trumpet's thoughts
An idea moving in the fingers
To become yourself when you are real
Saying to L.A. city of reluctant music:
Here is my fire, my holler and stomp
My insurgence

Lament

Buffalo Soldiers

ONCE THEY RODE TOGETHER
SLAVE AND INDIAN
ACROSS THE NUECES
AND BELOW THE RIO GRANDE

1.
First there is nothing
But the spirit
Left behind like a scent

Then there are the voices
Howls

Then the blue
Cavalry uniforms
The peaked caps

2.
Geronimo called them
Buffalo soldiers
It was the warrior
Naming his betrayer
He saw their strength
Like buffalo
And sensed the doom

3.
When they howled
It might have been
For all the years of dying
What makes a killer ride
Churning up the white dust
Chewing the corrosion
Screaming an old song

Once meant for God?
What makes the fear
Billow around him
In his own voice?

4.
It has been nearly two years
This pursuit
Geronimo eludes
The Sierra Madre holds him
How powerful is memory?
"You must not trust them
The land is not in them."
Now the mountains groan

5.
The patrol approaches
The border
That stretches ahead
Gouged in the cheek
Of the skin called Texas

Cattle will soon follow
The Buffalo Soldiers
And bankers, railroads
And the other gods
Of History
Now the men follow
The smell of death
The frontier

6.
They ride at night
When the sun goes down
Awaken with their shoulders
Aching against rocks
Their legs along the ground
Taut as telegraph wires
They reach for their rifles

Talk
Pick their teeth
With pocket knives
And dream of victory

Ruby Bates' Escape from Huntsville

RUBY BATES AND VICTORIA PRICE WERE THE TWO WHITE WOMEN WHO TESTIFIED
AGAINST THE SCOTTSBORO BOYS IN THE FAMOUS 1930S RAPE TRIAL. RUBY BATES
LATER RECANTED HER TESTIMONY AND WORKED FOR THE DEFENSE OF THE
BLACK TEENAGERS.

Oh, honey
The movies they show!
Sitting in the fertile
Mad dark of the cinema
After all the royal passions
Have faded and the credits roll
In the Jim Crow theater
Her lamenting chin
Is thrust into her breast
Eyes closed
Thinking
"What a place
Fucking Alabama
To be a queen of romance."

The cotton mill job ran out
And the vagrancy went to her head
She was ready to tell big lies
And see wild places on her own
She had a right
Seventeen years old and foreboding
Her back stooped with grime
Her chest whistling through her cigarette
Her nights spent loving
In the arms of a mill hand
Loving his coughing flesh
Sleeping in the dead wet night
Like a convict
Alert with longing
Waiting for the right freight train

This Depression earth
Ain't giving up nothing, sister
And politics has passed you by
If a man can do it
Why can't you?
Haul your treacherous flesh
Over the state line to Chattanooga
In a fire snorted by an engine
Going north or west or anywhere
Away from this prescription

She travels butch with Vicky Price
Who is older
With a body like the anxious clay
In drought time
Vicky is the hard one
Burning under her overalls
Dry from so many dollar bills
Stuffed up her crotch
Soaking up her tears

Ruby snares a whiskey-powered demon
In the hobo jungle
His mouth funnels fumes over her
Knowing she is an imposter
The idea of all that wiry cotton
Sprouting through the man's fly
Of her disguise
Is too much
She weathers the burst of his sour rain
The coins chime in her pocket
She snaps them inside
And swallows an appetite more aroused

Ruby finds Vicky at the hobo fire
And shares some boiling coffee
Their paltry words flicker
In the damp spring night
Down the track

They see the camp
Set up by the nigger bums
Waiting, too
For the same speeding boxcars
Scottsboro bound

Just an Illusion

Sometimes we have gestures in us
For generations
And some surprise
Some juncture of emergency
And opportunity
Pulls them out full fledged
Full blown
The way a magician
Whisks flowers out of nothing
And emptiness is suddenly
Vividly blooming

When that bouquet appears
It is no illusion
It is a sign
We have traveled
Into the next moment
There is no going back
No stuffing the blooms
Back up our sleeves

Verdell said
It never would have happened
If the man hadn't called them niggers
He should have just kept
Striding through the woods
Up the road to the sawmill
That way they could have made it home
From their date
Marred only by the cracker's cracker hood
He should have never not expected
The unexpected
Then turned and left his temple bared
To a spiked high heel

She jumped on the truck so fast
Her corsage fell on the piney ground
Her shoe hanging out of the racing window
Left its own red-petalled trail
Hell
It was 1940, Marshall, Texas
Far from the light of day
And that fool might track them down
If all that blood on his head
Ever convinced him
The niggers
Weren't just an illusion

1949 A.M.

FOR MY GRANDMOTHER, ZELLA

They have taken California from you, these black blustery strangers
In the world outside your window. The boom is everywhere.
The silence has been lost to these molasses mouth greetings
This rural tribe singing to the dawn, too grateful to understand
The shipyard isn't a job, the housing projects aren't home.
And where is your husband? Creole white face,
Shiny steel lunch bucket, secrets hugged to his chest
Along the trek with other morning faces
Things are better, the ship's hull ripped off in busy clouds
Is welcome work, the scrambling through tunnel lengths
Snowy with asbestos in the harbor wind is welcome work.
You don't know he's dying with a mechanic's precision
Imperceptibly.

You snap the blade
Of the Venetian blinds shut, contemplate the plague of dust
Shrug off anxiety. You and the children have followed him
Into a life of peacetime. Now the invaders are American
And Southern and California has grown big and rude,
Bursting its denim seams. Nothing will ever be the same.
The old Creole founders, and your father's barber shop,
The quiet classrooms where only the whites were rowdy,
Lutheran services grim and comforting, acres of orchards
Before they made downtown, your in-laws' sherry glasses
In the creaking china hutch, whispers about your mother
Who long ago passed, though everyone knew where she lived
In San Francisco with her new name and white husband,
The flagging gentility gone now.
When you met your husband
You were both children of West Oakland's innocence.
He wanted to be an artist; the walls of his boyish bedroom
Festooned with talent, the illicit cry of his heart
The seeds of his eyes flowering in the drawings

Taped everywhere. His sister yanked you
Down the hall to play in her girlish kingdom
But you never forgot the vision of those walls
The emblems of what a bright colored boy in a proper home
Could never be, his own man
Drawing the world a line at a time.

You close the door
On the horde of charcoals, pencils, draughts, photos, extra tools
The metric art your husband leaves behind
His imagination strewn about in barricades around the bed
Yours tucked somewhere in a pillow crease
After the riot of breakfast with seven children
You carry the baby to a neighbor's; a hint of relief, unacknowledged.
It's only been two months, but in this new world
Where the white women have gone back home to their children
So that their men can prepare the wars of the future
Mornings aren't a matter of choice.

Once back you dress in the windowless bathroom
Tying up your breasts with an improvised cotton and elastic
The harness in place, the cycle admonished with a tight tug
The milk that your baby won't have forced back to its source
The final gesture, pearly face powder that will curdle
In the factory steam
Outside the bus stop is a herald in the fog
Wide shoulders on your black thrift coat
Cross a lawn yellow with malnutrition
Your pressed straight hair, besieged by the dampness
Your auburn bangs, hot curled in front
Take the brunt of the Oakland spray.

The Maid's Night Out

She had swallowed poison
But thanks to the hospital
Emergency hose
Was gagged back to life
Lying in the testimony
Of her pumped out stomach
Her throat forever sour sore

She went to be a child again
In her mother's house
Going out in service every day
Coming back to a place that wasn't home
In the 1955 Jim Crow nights

The white ladies' kitchens shone
Even in her dreams
Her own Aladdin's Cave
Of yellow linoleum, silver chrome
White suds, blue windows
That might have held the sky

The cares of others
Stank worse than their toilets
The secrets of others
Wouldn't wear off with soap

All week she prayed
For Saturday night
It was the gold cross
On a chain kissing her cleavage
The amulet
She wore between her breasts

Oh, the glad fugitives

In the purple shadows
Of the party in a neighbor's living room
The record player
Saves them all from talking
So the truth could be spoken
In the dark

Someone clutches her around the waist
And pulls her into a Delta melancholy
At twenty she can't tell
If the golden bitterness and foam
Was the beer she'd swallowed?
Or the memory of wanting to die
Perhaps, she thinks, letting her belly go
Against the upbeat
It's the music
A guitar howl gone molten
In her throat

She is held tight against a shoulder
Red promise sings under her eyelids
A beer drips in one hand
A man sweating with love in the other, baby
Her knees sway to gratify
She knows what dancing is:
She can't get to her salvation
Unless he gets to his

Saturday night!
His arms wrap her like sheets
She surrenders
To the breaking wave of pleasure
Hopes it will last all week
This offbeat laughter
Her skin fragrant with escape

he Bay

A NORTH-BLOWING BREEZE, CAUGHT IN THE ACCIDENT OF THE GULF, SIGHS,
TRAPPED IN THE ANTIQUE SHADE OF A SHEDDED WHARF.

Galveston still boasts of its own slavery
In faded testimony of paint on its warehouses
"Largest Cotton Port in the World"
Auction blocks lie bloated in the depths
And the ghosts of screwed bales
Whistle through empty lazarettes
Pelican Isle is a thumb mark
On the pulse of the Gulf
Around it shrimp boats float a geometry
Of nets cast in an eager competition
With the birth rate of the sea

Across the Channel, Union Carbide grumbles,
Deity sheltered by the curve
Of Texas City's hard-working arm
Chemical vats surround it
Jupiter's moons in potent orbit

He walks as though he wants to leave
No record of his steps
Picking his way through ship dunnage
Scattered like souvenirs on jutting piers
It is slow traveling with him
And his memories
He would give everything
The gold watch, badge of retirement,
The cancer and T.B., everything
For the wooded catfish ponds of youth

He tells me of the symbols of his life
The twenty years of stiff shoes
Janitor's uniform and office waste

How the union came
The promotions scattering the tribe of janitors
To scale the Union Carbide vats all day
Wearing the banner of his maintenance job
Swathed tightly around his searing mouth
Dipping a measure of the chemicals to test
In the white laboratory
Gasping in the palpable air, glad
For the money and the position
And the end of segregation

Above our heads gulls and pelicans swerve
Strike the surface of the bay for food
Bucket up their squirming meals and swallow
Dashing heavenward
Then return to the brim of the Gulf

We, too, must eat
We feel our hunger watching the dive
And swoop of these birds
We have our lunch
Eaten delicately together
A respite, one of many
From the demanding air.

Martin Luther King

A summer of resurrection
Church in the South
Air littered with handkerchiefs
The faces of the congregation
Damp with fervor
Receptacles of the slow music of sacrifice
In the sermons of King
Rebel nailed to his own tribulation
A Christ bloody with betrayal
Inhaling thunder on the crucifix
Head hanging from a storm

Four murders
Children at worship bombed
Their deaths now the cornerstones
Of the black church
"Down payments on freedom," King said
King wept
Disciple of the bold carpenter
Ancient communist
Who tread along the fatal sea

A plaintive army marched
Singing its attack singing
Hosannas of red clay and longing
And the children's freedom
Writhing in the sharp jaws of dogs
The blood in the martyr's eye singing
And the youth with their hidden weapons
Their faith in fire
The hands of the elderly and righteous
Singing with applause
Singing we as a people
Shall get to the Promised Land

elsewhere

Mother Catherine

I came to New Orleans
Like everyone else
From nowhere

Now the hungry
The homeless
The lost
And all the splendid
Offspring of the Great Depression
Fill my Church of the Innocent Blood
With their prayers
For a rain of jobs

They believe
I can gain the ear of God
Who is nearer than Roosevelt
And more likely to respond

Under the church portico
The hundred carved, wooden saints
Witnessed my arrest

That night of silence
In the dank canal winds
I was betrayed as an abortionist
And rewarded with jail

It was then I swore
To outlive them
To outlast
Their catastrophes

The Creoles say:
Di moins qui vous laimens
Moins di vous qui vous yé
Tell me who you love
And I'll tell you who you are

My Congo
Stevedore
Sprung from levee mud
Crate scars on his back
Welts raised by coffee sacks, flour
Whiskey, sugar, cotton, spiraling
Banana crowns
At night he threw himself on me
Like cargo
His destiny of goods inside me
I love God
But here in jail
I miss my Congo more

The womb is the darkness
Of the earth's beginning
And like all mysteries
Should be left to bear
Its secrets in our lives

I saved the shipwrecked women
Who washed up on my table
Black or white
Or *femmes de coleur*
I held them in my arms
Bathed their faces
As they sweated out
Their dead passion

There at the outskirts
In the Church of the Innocent Blood
Even God trembled
At the desolation

When I kneel to pray
There are no candles
My cell black as the river
I kiss the cross and whisper the name
Of my sweet brother, Jesus
And our father
Who forsook us both

Downtown Kingston

The sweating walls of my hotel room breed mosquitoes
Orange juice washes down aki and sal' fish for breakfast
But does not transform me, curioser and curioser
From the lobby I mail postcards
Arawaks, Columbus landing
Maroons armed against their captors
The British triumphant with canon fire
Bustamante leading Independence
A hydroelectric dam, bauxite mine
The history of Jamaica in cartoons

I am supposed to be afraid here
The street corners are dangerous with wandering
Evangelists, pickpockets and madmen
Screaming about the way the world continues
Despite their predictions of its end

What threatens me is my own longing
Kingston matches my desperation
Trench Town where lies have left their trail
On a decorous porch under low-roofed government housing
An old woman shells peas, her skirt a cradle, gun across her knees

Downtown among the breadfruit stalls and ginger candy vendors
Rude hawkers and cheap goods merchants
Salt-scrubbed ruins and cultivated mansions
Wafts the sweet indifference of these survivors
The way of life in a black country
Where I am just another member of the family

It is hard to know what is worse:
Where we've come from or where we are headed
Were the suicides, deaths from smallpox
Rape killings, brandings, gun wounds, suffocation

In the slave holdings below deck on that journey across history's back
Intended to yield the ashen, drug-addled Rasta man outside Hope Gardens?
Or the sleek-haired matron in the gated Blue Mountains villa above
    the harbor?
Which one?

At the Bob Marley museum the lessons return to me
Of searing rum and dancing midnight ska
On the balls of our clever, student feet
Of songs as prophecy

Arguing into dawn about Mozambique, Chile, Vietnam
The geography of our youth
Taking to bed some quiet student who after fumbling love
Would read aloud the men whom our professors and our parents
Rejected out of hand
Devoted as we were to our chief discovery
That the world was miserable
And we were born in a guilty land

In our time, the gods sent Bob Marley
To leave a mark on Earth
Reminding us of the splendor
Available from within
He was incandescent
They allowed us that before recalling him
(The gods are jealous; whom they love they keep)
Here in Kingston are the artifacts of his soul:
Hushed whitewash
Lyrics painted near the ceiling, paraphrases of Christ
The sprawling grounds, banana trees, a moment of sea air
The sky above the place where sky began
The issue of the perfect sea, the bluest waters
Sudden thunder
Clouds twist themselves into summer dishrags
And wring down rain
Inside the shelter of the gift shop: posters, T-shirts, coffee mugs, key rings

The prophet's lanky face and dreadlocks on each and everything
For me there will be no souvenirs
Everything here is cheap
Everything except memory

Texas Town

There is money in this place
It blares
Like a rodeo tune
Everywhere
Kennedy is in
And the black people
Are relieved
It is as though
Some promise has been kept

In the neighborhood
Old Man who owns the corner store
Thrusts his gargoyle head
At the candy hungry children
To keep them from stealing

Everybody is trying
The best they can
Ma Dear among the toilets
In office buildings downtown
Willie Ruth working spells
In other people's kitchens
The little boy
Runs curly-headed
Through the Dallas wilderness

When Ma Dear's husband
Was a young man
They called him Hot Shot
And Dallas was too tame
For him
Hot Shot said
Even the white men in Dallas
Were small time

They shipped Hot Shot
To the Philippines
When the white men
Made their war
He drove trucks
In the jungle
Hauling supplies
To beat the Japanese
He had a hell of a time
Among those Army Negroes
Bourbon heavy at night
They sang a soldier chorus
It was the same old labor
As in Dixie
But now Hot Shot swung
The truck's gear shift
For himself
And for Democracy

He worked his soul thin
And willingly
It was his only aria
The war
Better than Dallas ever was
Or ever could be

Twenty years later
Hot Shot took off again
Kennedy was in
And the man got restless
They should have seen it coming
Ma Dear, Willie Ruth and the big-eyed boy
They should have know
When Hot Shot told them
That money made Dallas weak
Content to just stand there
Like a barkeep

Elbows on the counter
And the patience of greed
Waiting for an old fashioned shoot-em-up
To bring in business

What Keeps Mankind Alive?

A horde of thunder
Clouds
Flings insults
Against the hobbled people
In rain flooded streets
This is June in Dallas
A time for funerals
And storms
And one soul
Draped in a plastic
Garbage bag
His head in the embrace
Of a broken hat
Disgraces his feet
In the sewer

The rain ambushes us
We are caught in our shame
We cannot acknowledge
The assault
We look upon
The tar-infested earth
And name the roads
Call the cluster of naked
Pretenders skyscrapers
The old stone men
Belching their age into the sky
We call them factories
From the windshields
Of our cars
We believe we know
The framework
Of our lives

Is someone
Yet crying for his little one?
The bullet hole
In the window
Sunday dinner, chicken gravy
A child slumped over
Gristled bone
Lightning fury
The fleeing car
No one saw

Is someone
Yet wondering why his ancestor
Some poor captive
Howling like Job
Survived
From Africa's Windward Coast
To this shore of rain?

Even in the storm
Someone has to
Go to work
If all he has
Is a plastic garbage bag
For a rain coat
And a broken hat
To hold his head

Someone has to
Show up
For the swing shift
And walk inside the door
Of the old stone man
The factory
To worship in the temple
Of the ordinary
Someone has to believe

Watermelons in Mozart Place

I am far away from you in Maryland
Surrounded by a ceremony of crab eating
People settle their elbows on picnic tables
Skin smeared red hot with sauce
Palms open, tulips pointing at the cornflower sky
The table is piled high with the spicy armor of conquered crabs
The lips of the women grip spiky legs, emptying them
Of meat, trumpeting out their tangy juice
Strips of crab hang from their teeth
Hungering for you, there is no feast for me

The old black men in linen and suspenders dangle their heads backward
Toppling hats, risk falling off the edge of the world
The women slip sandals off secretly under the bench
In the lush Chesapeake ritual

This is another country being empty of you
It is strange and heightened by the bourbon odor
Around us
The men and women swill the very air
Make declarations that the heart is alive here
Music begins over loudspeakers
It is a rich invitation
One grey-haired woman
With spectacles and a gold tooth
Raises her paper cup like a castanet
Astonishing her husband
The afternoon itself runs for the safety of home

Ah, the moon's rise, its light through the piled clouds
Alongside the road called Mozart Place
A man packs up his stand of watermelons
Their easy hearts blood in a dream
He throws a canvas over them
And I can only think of night with you
Contracting into smaller and smaller
Darknesses

Ragtime on the Pipe Organ in Balboa Park

Summer in San Diego
The air light as jam
The organ player in shirt sleeves
Wields the tune of a colored man

Shadows tangle in the air
Flora hail from everywhere
To Eden's shame
We in the audience
Are just a dull plot
In the Garden

It has been one hundred years of forgetting
Scott Joplin manufactured these tunes
On the installment plan
Genius paid out in obscene rooms
Where drunks worshipped
Whores slept and the white people came
To hide from themselves

The children who took lessons from him
Crowds savoring his cornet playing in black-face bands
The black gentlemen of the Maple Leaf Club
His own peers commissioning his rags
The German master who taught him
No one knew that the minstrel
Would one day be King

Here in Balboa Park
Scott Joplin's story seem as distant
As the hopeful start of my marriage
Death came to both prematurely
The length from here to Joplin's home
In Missouri

Is not as far as my husband
Seated next to me on this stamped iron bench

In the Organ Pavilion
Donated by history's sugar barons
"To the people of all the world"
We are at the end of something,
It is over, the century, a way of life
Faith

No one ever knows what is going to happen
Scott Joplin's sweet mother
Bought her seven-year-old a piano
To bear him over countless seas
And help him plot the voyage
Between uncharted notes

Here the sun's dusting laces the trees
No amount of rushing by the player
Through the ragtime's minuet, the stride
No surfeit of summer cheer
Can hide the serenade of grief in this music
The weeping we refuse to hear

Soon I will leave my husband
The known world shall disappear
It is possible I shall live as a failure
Or else compose a sound never heard before

Scott Joplin made a world of grace
Others were not ready for
He knew what we must learn:
There is sadness everywhere
And beauty, too, everywhere

City

ag Lady

Earth
That old woman
Has shoved her shopping cart
Under the freeway
And stained her fingers
With the ink of tears
She lives in a muttering shadow
Knit cap over her ears
Black skin branded by fear

The refuse of the human heart
Is piled up in her cart
Gathered from those
Who have stopped waiting
For the promise
In the locked laboratories
In the arsenals
In the high places
They have prepared her funeral
There will be no music
Not even the blues
And no one left to grieve

Pilgrim on Skid Row

Her back wide as a barge
Head in a fedora
Bulging paper bag
In her motherless arms

The sun begins its drive
There is no place to sit
She's a nomad walking
To keep her equilibrium

She passes where the wretches stand
Among the herds of traffic
Mercy is here
A gladiola in her hand

Proverb

We cannot shut out
The perpetual war
We call
The city

When you love
All rushes in

There is no door
Wider
Than the heart

On Hiroshima Day

In Little Tokyo
A Koto player
Sits in a black robe
And steel-toed shoes
On stage

He sings

His stalwart voice
Bolsters the sky
Saves music for the world

Pentecost

FOR MY FATHER

I have my faith
But look what has come of it
Where does a man go
In defiance?
Where can he be humble
Only before God?

The polite church
shuns
The old, brutal stories
But they are what made me
Through them God spoke to me
Saying, Be a hero
Take your stone and aim it
At the mountain
Cut down your foes
Make them bleed
So that life can become
What you dream

And God stood me well
As a boy against my father
When the stern aristocracy
Of our church building generations
Failed in him
In the days when my mother
Had only me as her defender
Until he was not dead drunk
Just dead
God stood me well
When I left childhood
To come to California
Amid hosannas

Of the football fans
In my student glory on the field
God stood me well
On the aircraft carrier from Hawaii
To the blood zones of Korea
And back to a country
Not sure of its beliefs
The beast of history
Not yet tamed
The whites fighting change
And my people who made it
God stood me well
Through strikes and union talks
Three jobs at a time
The fragile lives of my innocent children
And the innocent life of my fragile wife

My faith was built on nothing less
Than the unexpected loveliness
Of life
The goodness I never dared
To want
The city that grew up around me
And my beautiful neighbors
The wealth everywhere during the war
That dying boys in Vietnam made possible
My own son too young to go
Though if he had been threatened
With the draft
I would have broken both his legs
To keep him home

The day the radio in the warehouse
Delivered the blow –
King killed in Memphis –
Was the day that the orbit
Of our Earth shifted
And the city slid into the sea
A thousand men

Those of us who knew
What God had meant
In the book of Acts
When He said,
That "Suddenly there came a sound
From heaven as of a rushing mighty wind"
Why, all of us walked out the gaping
Warehouse door and stood as mutes
In open air
No longer brother,
Shop steward, friend
We left for home
Each with his firearm
In the passage of flight
Not knowing from whom
We were protecting our families
The whites at work
Who had watched us go
Or the rioters
As the city burned that night

So, I am not surprised
When we are told
Of the plant closing
I stand on my dingy spot
And the work day begins
They tell me: This is the Seventies
Another beginning
But death comes
Before the Resurrection
And a man never knows
How to react to the news
He is going to die
He loses genius then
It is as if I have no mother
No father, no children, no wife
The factory has spawned me
And never lets me forget
That I am alive

Not in all the overworked
Regions of my body

Yet I hope still
For a memorial
A life shaped finally into
A weapon
Used by my ferocious God
All day I wait
For some event some surprise
The storming of the factory walls
Seven trumpet blasts
But night once again
Finds me in the parking lot
Wondering how to get home
The waste of the harbor refineries
Burning in the abandoned night
Their flames
Leaping above my head

Notes on a Storefront Church

Preacher strides through the urban shambles
Wafting the holy scents of aftershave and whiskey
The factory pays his money
But this is his real job
Finding the pitch of his soul
In the long wail of Wednesday nights

Louisiana man on crutches
Talks of a polio childhood
Women gather on the weary concrete
In the best suits welfare can buy
Children chase street cats and the shadows
Of trees

Light from the door sprawls across the sidewalk
Night brings a rumor of industry downwind
Slaughterhouses
Still alive in the Christian dark

Organ tremolos reach outside
Worshippers pull up anchor
Hushed expectant as Christmas morning
Go indoors
Merge with the light
Leave the bloody air
To the meatpackers on swing shift

This Morning

This morning speaks to us
And we feel what a shape we are
Mammal and upright, and worse, sinner
We visitors welcomed this morning
To Rock of Faith Missionary Baptist Church
In the city's trembling heart
Where it is foretold
The shouting good time that will be had this morning

This morning, this morning the sun circles
Around our heads through
The patchwork glass of windows
In the rumble of old wood
This morning

Somehow this morning holds its breath
For the heart to be heard
Beating in these pews
And when the preacher's wife claims the piano
Its keys beat, too

It is the beat that sounds everywhere in this city
When the breath is held
For the heart to be heard
Out of the pavement chase
Out of the warehouse shoes
Out of the truck growl
And the car grimace
And the hammer hands
That reach for the truth
In a day, its hours
Out to the ocean edge
With its mouth calling
From the berths and piers

And the dock pounding
And the ship impatience
And the body rocking loose
Into the wind dash
Into the lung gulp
Into the rain drive
Out of the blue born
Out of the cetacean dark

And the voices of the choir
Don't relent this morning
This morning that has lifted
The entire world and spun it
On the long note of a gospel solo
And there is life
All the way from our sun flamed heads
To our feet
And beneath our feet
Beneath even the floor
There is life
Pushing ahead through the deep
Which it knows
And which the voices of the choir
Take us back to

This morning, this morning we remember
What it is we hold silently in our throats
Until it leaps out full volume
From the dark below
And we clench our eyes shut
And shake our heads from side to side
Because it has surfaced
Over there in the far pew
In the first scream
In the legends of blood and night
In the memory of sanctuary
When life dangled by its neck
From the pain of slavery everywhere

Even the sky rained it
And we built a small shelter of wood
Against the downpour
Against the horror that was human
And was made by humans
This morning we remember
Why we are here
The way we tried for one Sunday moment
To find a voice and
And call it divine

Generosity

The city talks
To keep from making sense

Your face blazes
In the wild red leaves

The miles between us burn

Walking
I take the corners
On hips forced apart by love

You won't be coming back

The pavement is kind
It accepts the weight of my futility

The Economy of Love

Skittish as the stock market she rises
To his doorstep
Wades through confetti circulars
Discarded trades at her feet

The glazed belly of the door
Mirrors her longing
Paper secrets breathe through
Slim metal gills in the mailbox

And there, under the sweet order
Of his name
The fetching arithmetic of his apartment
The buzzer summons him
A gamble in futures

$\mathcal{G}$oing For Barbecue II

Night is for solitary fools like me
Foot on the gas pedal, searching for home
Going south on Crenshaw
Until, in the distance, the neon pig dances on the roof
Heralding the corner barbecue joint

Some people have actually given up on barbecue
They say they are too healthy
Or the neighborhood where you go to pick up your order
Is too violent
Or, they are waiting for celebrity basketball players
To open a new soul food restaurant with pink linen
Tablecloths on Melrose Avenue
They believe they have come too far
From the pungent legacy
Of caste and shame emerged from Slave Quarters
Nigger Alleys Vaqueros Wetback Rancheros Coolie Railroad Labor and
Red Indians
In America's meanest parts

Case in point:
In 1947 Richard Wright ran all the way to Paris
Because the Sheriff of Nottingham wanted him out of Sherwood Forest
It wasn't a good era for Robin Hood in America –
Not if he wanted to buy a home, send his daughters to school,
Walk the street, ride a cab, speak the truth, tell a lie,
Be called Mister instead of boy – not if he was black at the same time

Richard Wright tried settling down
But he couldn't obey the rules of exile, either, not even
In the city of lights. So he surprised himself
By traveling all over the world and writing books
Angry, eloquent love letters to America
Returned unopened

Restless every time back in Paris
He had to face his longing for the unattainable
A slab of ribs
Drenched in the substance of desire and smoking like the train whistle
Heart of the blues
He couldn't stop talking about it, his hunger ringing like a bell
He never wanted to see America again, except
For the corner barbecue shack he remembered
Perfuming Harlem's dim highways
Existentialism was nothing compared to these dimensions
Of suffering
Although sometimes Camus – himself
Yearning for the savory breezes and tangy streets of Algeria –
Sometimes Camus could understand

I believe it is possible to die of barbecue deprivation
To be so far away from the people who gave you life
That, no matter what you eat, how fine it is, you cannot be fulfilled
And you waste away like a bar of soap in water
Gone to oblivion, only a residue of memory left behind

Some people insist that because he betrayed them both
In the cold war lust for the prizes of life
Either the CIA or the Communists
Poisoned Richard Wright
With the ingredients in his own kitchen
But they are wrong
He died of heartbreak
What killed him was wanting more than anything those two praying
Hands of white bread wrapped around hot links
In the sauce that brings tears of homesickness to your lost eyes
Leaving his enemies meant leaving his people, too
His people who transcended every insult beating rape murder lynching
    prison
And created a country called America that nobody would recognize
If it wasn't for them
More than wealth, love, kindness, the safety of children, peace on Earth
What we want
Is to cross the border under night's camouflage

In pursuit of the sweet fiery taste we call home
It's not a place we're going to, but a feeling
Driving south on Crenshaw into deep territory
Car shaking to the radio's loud rumble, the gift of a bass note
Sent by Africa a long, long time ago

Bliss

Outwitting the Night

In the bedroom cavern
Of school night darkness
Sam Cooke rescued me

Eternity in ear plugs
My body a dream
Made by my own hands

My father's gift
Of the transistor radio
For sixth-grade graduation
Put to use he never planned

Ghosts swooning
At love's distilled melody
I wasn't too young to understand

Early to bed
My mother said
The lights died

I traveled alone
With my first love in flight
Sam Cooke's voice
For me and me alone
Outwitting the night

War Games

Those nights we lied
Telling our parents
This was no mixed party
Just us girls sleeping over
Wearing all that machinery to bed
To curl our straightened hair
Walking with a hive of bees
Between our legs
From too much cologne
Sprayed in our shrubs
Hauling our hungry
Pajamas
Up our gangways

We
Believed in the boys
Without them we were just
Unlit matches
With no surface
To ignite upon
We needed them to flame
And once that
Brightness vanished
We were simply burnt tinder
Dead

We believed
That our fifteen
Year old lives
Would wait until we
Caught up with them
It was the way
Aretha made us feel
Believing in Dr. Feel Good

Believing these skirmishes
Would be remembered
As love

And we would go to them
In someone's borrowed Impala
Windows open
The world a windy back seat
With a fearless radio
Embraced
By our voices
Driving from our own
Protected camp
We would proclaim the manifesto
Of a do right all day woman

We arrive
The wind abandons us
We hear the jukebox
Blast
Inside the house
This is not an ambush
We know the boys
Are waiting for us
The bayonets in their pants
At the ready

In the dark room
The forty-five record slips
Down the spindle whispering
"Do you want to dance?"
The irresistible
Click
Of the slow music
On the phonograph
The weapons are drawn
We aim ourselves at them

For Langston

From the first
Bold
Blind kick
Against the womb
I knew
You would fight
Your way
To the light

Your face stamped
With the cosmic surprise
Of my father's face

At three years old
Already ancient and wise
You tell me "I'm not crying,"
Just "putting the tears
Out of my eyes"

Childhood
Dies hard
Wanting to help
It was my job to fail
I watched you
From the border
Of my own country
Where you once lived, too

Sorrow
Belongs to those of us
Who are left behind
Namesake
Of the poet
Son
That sweetest sound
The name now
Of a man

The Glow of a Rose

FOR MY MOTHER

And if my life is like the dust
Oooh, that hides the glow of a rose
What good am I?
Heaven only know.
—CLYDE OTIS, THIS BITTER EARTH

You loved us
You loved us the way you loved sleep
The nights you worked graveyard at the Post Office
You stood at our beds
As we abandoned you
Pushing off to the far country
Waving over blithe shoulders
At your loss
Leaving it up to you to salvage
The dreams we left behind
When you closed the front door behind you
It had grown faint, the memory
Of dancing on the night's wide, dark floor

Life turned on the lights at the party
Scattering the innocents
There you were, face to face with our father
No one was young in those days
The world had already survived too much
You made the unbreakable pact
From the foundation of the world
Grim, joyous gift to your children
One head, two faces, Janus, Parent God
The sun and moon embodied in each other
Interchanging in the marriage dance

Who was the girl everybody said

Made her own music with laughter?
The blonde, eldest girl of eight
Who kicked the rugs out of mind
Let ecstasy spread under her feet
Wrapped her legs around that good soul music
And rode

On school mornings we awakened
To your humming Dinah Washington
A glamorous, obsolete tune
With a broken bottle edge and a hint of strings
Insisting something about love
Something about love
The bathroom plumbing whined
You spit your toothpaste
To its destiny
And gargled a song
From when music
Still meant something to you

Going for Barbecue I

Back then we knew when it was time
To sample the authentic gifts of the ghetto
As exiles we knew the moment well
The yearning for hot links, the blackened slab of ribs
The potato salad only made in dreams

Our parents navigated the journey
Over the Bay Bridge, that mammoth bird
Shimmering wings of ocean at its sides
We approached the city electric
With it canopy of wires, buses hooked up to God

Back then the wires were pulled tight
Around San Francisco's veins
Fillmore was where the needle entered
And triggered the jukebox
Jimi Hendrix at the Fillmore Auditorium
James Brown, the vocal chords of radios
Strung on store transoms, Doo Wop quartets
On history's street corners

Back then, we sniffed the charbroiled air
Of the fragrant temple before we saw it
The bum sleeping decorously
In the gutter, the long, hungry lines
On the pavement
Outside Leo's Barbecue Shack

Going home we children sat
With our heads bowed over the Eucharist
The pork flesh with its oily wine
Seeping through brown paper take-away

We didn't mind, oh no, we loved it
Smelling, smelling like a rib joint
Wafting above the bay

Childhood Visions of Creativity

Father humming afternoon
Garage blues
Tempo of the tool box
The uses of shadows
The day the world was made

Mother releasing backyard
Linen from bondage
Sheets flee their clothespins
Shreds of sun painted on
Masterpieces of light

Baseball on the Radio in the Backyard

Tennis shoes bruise the lawn
It's a game
We don't know what it's called
On the radio a high fly ball
Sails out of the mythic park
Joy smells of green grass

Illumination

Our traffic battered car
Rolls over the rough asphalt
Into the church parking lot
My father stills the machine
My mother sighs with the triumph
Of arrival
They rouse us
Their children in the back seat
Heavy eyed and homesick
For our beds

Inside
The sun slides itself
Back through the church windows
After having gone prodigal
During the night
The light
From the stained glass
Cuts like ice
In the church pews
Even the old ladies
In fur coats shiver
We children rub our hands
To keep them warm
And watch our breath
Make its jail break
From our mouths

The old sanctuary
Is experienced at winter
Built as it was against the cold
The wood creaks
Bodies settle into seats
The congregation whispers

The organ is pumped into life
The choir rustles
A flock of birds
Restless for feeding

The hymn finds its way
Out of the desolation of its beginning
As the men's choir sings
My father's tenor solo rises
Above the old slave chorus
That rhythms on
Until its end
And the silence
Its tone
Is suspended still
Still
Still
In that air

About the Author

Susan D. Anderson teaches, speaks and writes about African American history, politics, and culture, with an emphasis on California and the West. She is the managing director of "L.A. As Subject," an association of libraries and archives hosted by the University of Southern California. She has been a Visiting Professor at Pitzer College in Claremont and is a Contributor to the Los Angeles Times Sunday Opinion. In addition to her poetry, she has published articles, essays and short fiction.